FORGE FORWARD

YOUR FREEDOM IS
HARD EARNED

JONATHAN MAYO

FREEDOM

Freedom begins where compliance ends. Freedom represents the courage to think and act independently, to cultivate personal growth unhindered by external control. It is a mindset of self-ownership that exercises one's faculties to take purposeful action despite barriers and limitations.

True freedom acknowledges the liberty of others. It persists through struggle and transcends adversity through indomitable determination. Freedom depends on the individual strength to accept consequences and responsibility for one's choices and is predicated upon the individual's decision to bear up under the weight of their discipline-born responsibilities.

Freedom grants individuals' sovereignty over their lives. It unleashes personal potential and guards the human spirit against restraint. Freedom catalyzes creativity, issue resolution, and the autonomous capacity to define one's own purpose. It echoes the irrepressible life force that strives forward under adversity and expands in proportion to resistance.

WE ARE ONLY AS STRONG, AS WE ARE INDIVIDUALLY FREE.

ADMINISTRATIVE PAGE

First published in the United States by Forge Publications.

FORGE FORWARD:
YOUR FREEDOM IS HARD EARNED

Copyright © 2023 by Jonathan Mayo

https://jonmayo.com

The Library of Congress Cataloging-in-Publication Data is available upon request.

ISBN 979-8-9876422-4-5 (paperback)

Our books may be purchased in bulk for promotional, educational, or business use. Please contact us at https://jonmayo.com

DEDICATION

TO FREEDOM.

GRATITUDE

TO EACH WARRIOR THAT HAS PAID
THE ULTIMATE PRICE TO SAFEGUARD
FREEDOM, TO MY BRIDE, AND
TO THOSE WHO CONTINUE TO
SUPPORT ME AND MAKE THIS WORK
POSSIBLE, THANK YOU.

RESILIENCE

BY JONATHAN MAYO

If you can wake before the darkness lifts,
And forge your mind as the dawn light drifts,
If determination is your morning song,
Growing stronger with each day long.

If you can hold the course when storms arise,
See opportunity with open eyes,
Transforming trials into lessons clear,
March on, WayMaker, cast aside fear.

Reject excuses, stay steadfast on the path,
Accountable, in kindness, not in wrath,
Live with integrity in every deed,
Speaking truth, embracing every need.

If you can lead amidst the chaos swell,
Anchor hope, through each trial and knell,
If you dare to love, despite its pain,
Blessing even those who disdain.

If neither heights nor depths can sway your sight,
From cherished aims glowing ever bright,
If you treasure moments, each a precious gem,
Pouring your heart into the now, not when.

If you lift those who stumble and fall,
Band together, with one and all,
Champion dreams once deemed too far,
Raising freedom's banner, your guiding star.

Resiliently daring, facing fear's assault,
Always trying, in failures, find no fault,
If you toil, bleed, weep for better days,
Yours will be the life that forever sways.

The hourglass counts moments well spent,
For you live with purpose, never relent,
Beyond yourself, you shape destiny's frame,
Enduring honor will extol your name.

And what is more, you may ask,
A WayMaker you are, in this noble task,
With a heart that's brave, strong, and vast,
Living intentionally, your legacy will last.

FOREWORD

In "Be Relentless," I extended an invitation and provided a flexible framework to transition from a state of dissatisfaction to a life of purpose, one that resonates with your deepest values. At the heart of this transformation is the WayMaker—a person who turns obstacles into opportunities through intentional action and unwavering resilience, characterized by 'Sisu', a Finnish concept for stoic determination. "Be Relentless" offers the roadmap to becoming that WayMaker.

Now, with "Forge Forward: Your Freedom is Hard Earned," I delve deeper into the journey that evolves from personal growth to the endurance required as we strive to empower others as WayMakers.

This book is a candid reflection of my path toward living these principles, capturing where I stand currently in the continuous process of personal application. By sharing this, I hope to broaden the invitation, encouraging us to press on together, to forge forward from the trials of initial adversity into the challenges of being world builders—those who create, fortify, and invigorate their families, communities, and the world at large.

While I am contemplating the title "Fellowship of Freemen" for a subsequent work, it remains a concept in motion, one that will develop further through continued action and must, therefore, wait.

For now, I am profoundly thankful to have you accompany me on this next phase of our collective journey toward becoming the best versions of ourselves for the benefit of others. Although the path is arduous, we find purpose in the progress we make.

THANK YOU FOR CONTINUING TO JOURNEY WITH ME.

CHAPTER 1:

FROM EMBRACING OUR MORTALITY TO CREATION AND CONNECTION

Throughout life there are concepts that remind us of our mortality, ideas that urge us to live, to create, and to connect. Born from stoicism, the ideas Memento Mori and Memento Viveri lay the foundation to aid us in remembering our fleeting mortality and therefore to live it fully. I have worked to expand on these ideas by focusing on two additional critical elements that I believe are fundamental to the work at hand. The power of creating value, Memento Crear (Remember to Create), and connection, Memento Conectare (Remember to Connect). Together, these ideas form a mosaic that depicts the full spectrum of a purpose-driven existence. They are reminders that serve as the cornerstones of the WayMaker Philosophy, guiding us not merely to exist but to lead lives rich with intention, creation, and connection.

MEMENTO MORI: THE URGENCY OF NOW

Memento Mori, "remember that you must die," is an ancient practice that has been a part of my reflections and the foundation of my book "Be Relentless." It is not a call to dwell on the inevitable end but a catalyst to seize the fleeting moments with purpose and passion.

In a noisy world full of distractions, Memento Mori breaks through as an ever-present call to live presently, casting aside the superficial. It heightens our senses and urges us to soak in life's beauty and meaning while we have this fleeting chance.

At its core, it is about making every decision, every action count, because our time here is limited. It is a call to push beyond mediocrity, to strive for excellence in every venture, because the tick of the clock is unrelenting.

MEMENTO VIVERI: THE CELEBRATION OF LIFE

Once awakened by Memento Mori's reminder of temporality, Memento Viveri, "remember to live," beckons us to drink deeply from life's richness. It is an exhortation to thrive rather than just survive. The practice of celebrating life breeds resilience and determination to press on amid adversity. It enables the embodiment of "Sisu"— extraordinary perseverance even under immense pressure with seemingly insurmountable odds.

Rejoicing over life is a choice. Everyone will die, but you do not need to die complaining. Even among hardship, we can uncover profound meaning when we actively engage with each moment and identify the elements within it that are gifts worth cherishing.

MEMENTO CREAR: THE POWER OF CREATION

"Remember to create" flows out of enlightened living. Unshackled from distractions, aware of fleeting time, we naturally overflow into the impulse of creation. To create is to emulate life's Creator, harnessing one's skills to serve a greater good.

Everyone has creative capacity waiting to be nurtured and deployed. This can transpire through launching new initiatives or reimagining tired systems. It may happen by nurturing personal growth or pouring wisdom into others. Creativity is the spark turning dreams into realities that outlive us, and from my estimation the only inexhaustible resource known to humankind is our ability to create value.

MEMENTO CONECTARE: THE IMPERATIVE OF CONNECTION

Finally, at its core, life is not fully lived until connected. A life spent alone quickly grows cold, no matter the miles traveled. It is sharing the adventure that ignites fire within our souls.

Memento Conectare, "remember to connect," awakens us to our shared nature. It reminds us that though each journey is unique, we need one another. Community amplifies joy and eases sorrows. When disconnected, we drift aimlessly; when linked arm in arm and heart in heart, we march forward empowered.

This is the powerful movement beckoning us forward. Anchoring traditions paired with exhilarating promise, we stand on the shoulders of giants. Now we must connect them together, and expend our lives in pursuit of creating, connecting, and living to the best of our abilities. For regardless of faith, belief, or creed, the steps that follow our last breath are a mystery and adventure.

THE TIME TO LIVE IS NOW.

CHAPTER 2:

IDEOLOGICAL ALCHEMY

As we progress on the WayMakers journey of relentless self-improvement, it is useful to ground our efforts in a robust methodology based on the alignment of our inner world with our outer expression. I refer to this deliberate process as "Ideological Alchemy" - utilizing the metaphor of alchemists transforming base materials to gold - but in this case we deliberately transform our thoughts, speech patterns, behaviors and ultimately our identity to embody our highest personal ideals.

This process of inner alignment echoes the familiar alchemical quest to transform base metals into gold. But instead of physical materials, we are refining the substance of our consciousness, painstakingly distilling our thoughts and words until they crystallize into purified action.

The idea of Ideological Alchemy involves recognizing the self-amplifying cycle connecting our beliefs, speech, and actions. Our thoughts and internal perspectives guide our words. Our spoken language reinforces mental patterns while also spurring behavior aligned with embedded ideologies. Behaviors repeated enough become ingrained habits and identity traits.

This self-perpetuating loop highlights why aligning our thoughts, speech and actions is critical for meaningful change. When synchronized, they facilitate positive transformation. When fragmented, they remain at odds, undermining progress.

Thus, Ideological Alchemy is the practice of initiating controlled positive change at the level of thought and speech to transform behaviors and identity with intentional consistency over time.

THE POWER OF WORDS

"We cannot evolve faster than our language. The edge of being is the edge of meaning, and somehow, we have to push the edge of meaning. We have to extend it."

- TERENCE MCKENNA

I love this idea as it captures how our ability to grow is intertwined with the words we use, both our private self-talk and public utterances. Our language and metaphors quite literally shape and constrain how we interface with reality. Consequently, the vocabulary and verbal patterns we employ end up limiting our perceptual boundaries and behavior unless we consciously expand them. Given that we cannot know that which we are unaware of, this concept encourages us to reidentify obstacles as limitations in our linguistics, which therefore limit our ability to respond positively. Given this, when facing obstacles that we do not know how to overcome, we must seek knowledge that is new to us and update our language accordingly, and in so doing we update our capabilities and ourselves.

Ideological Alchemy fully embraces this relationship between speech and personal evolution. Our thoughts vocalized establish the playing field upon which we change and develop. To transcend our current selves, we must enrich and upgrade the cognitive models encoded in our linguistic choices and narratives.

As we deconstruct restrictive vocabulary and construct empowering mental frameworks, we drive the transformation of identity itself. Our speech provides the trajectory to exceed perceived constraints.

EMPIRICAL FOUNDATIONS

Practices within Ideological Alchemy are strongly supported by psychology and neuroscience. Frameworks like mindfulness meditation and empowering self-talk empirically influence neural patterns while improving motivation and self-esteem. Techniques from Neurolinguistic Programing (NLP) that alter language habits also facilitate positive personal changes.

The key insight across these modalities is that intentionally evolving our thought and speech patterns can gradually yet markedly modify behavior. While avoiding mystical claims to turn consciousness into substantive gold, through this philosophical discipline of inner alignment, we can synchronize the outputs of action to manifest our ideal selves—fully realizing our potential by sculpting an identity built with intention.

CHAPTER 3:

THE WAYMAKER CODE – A CREED FOR INTENTIONAL LIVING

The WayMaker Philosophy is not just a passive means of perceiving the world. Rather it is for the "practioners", the doers of deeds, those who step into the great arena of life and do not leave until they have drawn their last breath. Given this, it is helpful to create a structured means through which we can perceive the world, and then to transform that lens into an action-oriented proclamation that we can live out each day (ideological alchemy).

In this chapter, we will explore the WayMaker Code - ten value-focused guidelines designed to optimize and actualize our potential. We will see how this Code takes shape as a daily proclamation - transforming high-level ideas into a personal creed for intentional living. I will also share my own adapted daily meditation ritual to model how you can internalize this Code into your identity and decision making with consistency and purpose.

The goal of this Code is not to constrain but to inspire. It is a framework for liberation applied through our thoughts, words, and actions. When not just espoused but embodied, these principles push us to expand the boundaries of what we believe possible - bridging the gap between present reality and future potential.

THE WAYMAKER CODE – AN OVERVIEW

Live Intentionally - Align your daily actions with your deepest values, consistently striving for personal excellence and meaningful impact.

Cultivate Curiosity - Seek the thrill of the unknown with eager questions and an open mind.

Pursue Wisdom - Nurture a growth mindset, relentlessly seek knowledge and insight, learn from both success and failure.

Uphold Truth - Prioritize forthrightness, openly admit your mistakes, and foster integrity in every action and interaction.

Be Relentless - Constantly chase your ambitions, overcome obstacles with unwavering tenacity and enduring resolve.

Forge Courage - Face challenges head-on. Bravery is a choice. Embrace discomfort and push beyond your limits to grow stronger.

Embody Sisu - Foster resilience in the face of adversity. Lead by example and transform challenges that come your way into opportunities for growth.

Foster Unity - Cultivate compassion and seek understanding. Together, we are stronger, and our progress is amplified when we work together.

Champion Freedom - Freedom comes at a price. Take responsibility for safeguarding it and dedicate efforts to cultivate a world where liberty flourishes.

Build Legacy - Invest your efforts in actions that resonate beyond the present. Create lasting, positive impact.

Now that you have read the code, let us transform it into a proclamation. Note how the subtle changes in the linguistics of this code help us to perform "ideological alchemy" and transform static statements into action-based proclamations.

THE WAYMAKER PROCLAMATION – IDEOLOGICAL ALCHEMY AT WORK

I Live Intentionally - I align my actions with my deepest values, consistently striving for personal excellence and meaningful impact.

I Cultivate Curiosity - I seek the thrill of the unknown with eager questions and an open mind.

I Pursue Wisdom - I nurture a growth mindset, relentlessly seeking knowledge and insight, and learning from both success and failure.

I Uphold Truth - I prioritize forthrightness, openly admit my mistakes, and foster integrity in every action and interaction.

I Am Relentless - I consistently chase my goals, overcoming obstacles with unwavering tenacity, and enduring resolve.

I Forge Courage - Knowing that bravery is a choice, I choose to take decisive action in the face of adversity. I embrace discomfort and push beyond my current limits to grow stronger.

I Embody Sisu - I foster resilience in the face of adversity. I lead by example and transform challenges into opportunities for growth.

I Foster Unity - I cultivate compassion and seek understanding. Together, we are stronger, and our progress is amplified when we work together.

I Champion Freedom - Freedom comes at a price. Therefore, I take responsibility for safeguarding it and dedicate efforts to cultivate a world where liberty flourishes.

I Build Legacy - I invest my efforts in actions that resonate beyond the present, creating lasting, positive impact.

With the subtle linguistic shift from instructive language to action oriented, radically responsible, precise language, not only does the code come to life, but we come to life with it by adopting the ideas presented.

This proclamation is designed to provide a starting place for your daily meditation, a discipline that we will explore now.

DAILY MEDITATION - A DISCIPLINED RITUAL

As discussed in "Be Relentless", as well as in chapter 2, there is immense power in intentionally adjusting our thoughts by carefully selecting the manner in which we speak. Given this, I have adopted the discipline of centering myself each day by conducting a focused meditation upon waking.

I conduct this meditation by proclaiming to myself, either silently or aloud depending on my environment, the following. Given my world view, and the unreligious faith that I hold, I view it deeply intimate personal ritual, that allows me to ground myself in the humility of my finite mortality, acknowledging that there is much beyond my understanding, while daring to relentlessly forge forward.

I hope that by presenting and exploring my daily meditation ritual, it will aid you in developing your own. Sharing this exposes me to your scrutiny, yet the risk of judgment or any ill-willed conversation that might arise from my openness is outweighed by the potential it has to illustrate the powerful impact of incorporating the WayMaker Code into your daily affirmations. This could significantly further your transformation into a WayMaker, as you strive to create substantial value and build strong community.

Note: A templated version of this daily meditation ritual is provided at the end of this book, in the Putting It Into Action section, to help begin cultivating these intentional practices in your own life.

MY DAILY MEDITATION RITUAL – AN EXAMPLE TO EXPLORE

"Lord, I lay down the troubles and burdens of my heart, the fears, and insecurities, so that you may remove them by your own hand and instruct my actions. Please forgive me for where I have sinned and help me to grow stronger and healthier so that I may better serve You; purify me, so that I may walk with You and receive your Spirit; please pour out Your favor and Your Holy Spirit on my house and me. Please help me to think, deeply, intuitively, and well; please grant me wisdom and insight far beyond my mortal form. Please grant me the courage to change what is in my control, the serenity to accept that which is not, and the wisdom to discern between the two. Please enable further levels of freedom, empowerment, influence, purpose, and peace. Please teach me how to give of myself open and freely, and how to receive in kind. Please safeguard my family, myself, and my mind. I commit myself to You Lord, and I commit my works to You Lord so that all that I do may honor You.

I proclaim the following as truth so that Your will may be done, and that I may honor You:

I Live Intentionally - I choose to be present in each moment. I align my actions with my deepest values, consistently striving for personal excellence and meaningful impact. I hold on to the outcome loosely but hold to the path fervently. I rejoice in doing what others refuse to do, so that I may do that which others are incapable of doing. And as I stand in the gap, I call others forward and equip them to do the same.

I Cultivate Curiosity - I seek the thrill of the unknown with eager questions and an open mind.

I Pursue Wisdom - I nurture a growth mindset, relentlessly seeking knowledge and insight, and learning from both success and failure.

I Uphold Truth - I speak the truth with deliberate intentionality, so that each word precisely relays the meaning and value that I intend for it to relay, and so my yes means yes and my no means no. Furthermore, I prioritize forthrightness, openly admitting my mistakes, and fostering integrity in every action and interaction. I remember that what I do speaks so loudly that no one can hear what I say, and what I do in private, is written on my soul. Given this I pause and weigh my actions so that my decisions make me stronger.

I Am Relentless - I exercise extraordinary violence of action, consistently chasing my goals, I overcome obstacles with unwavering tenacity, and enduring resolve.

I Forge Courage - Knowing that bravery is a choice, I choose to take decisive action in the face of adversity. I embrace discomfort and push beyond my current limits to grow stronger. I choose to lead well.

I Embody Sisu - I foster resilience in the face of adversity. I lead by example and transform challenges into opportunities for growth.

I Foster Unity - I cultivate compassion and seek understanding. I respond with intention. I believe that together, we are stronger, and our progress is amplified when we work together. I choose LOVE and I breathe in gratitude. I seek to cultivate a vibrant life of love with Lindsey, my bride, and pursue her with fresh eyes, elation, and wonder. I cherish her and choose to love her more deeply, today, and I discipline my mind and body such that she is my only source of satisfaction, otherwise I maintain my strength. I cultivate control over the expression of my emotions, thoughts, and my voice as I instruct my sons, through my example and my word. I choose to cherish my time with them and remember that each moment is a gift.

I Champion Freedom - Freedom comes at a price. Therefore, I take responsibility for safeguarding it and dedicate efforts to cultivate a world where liberty flourishes.

I Build Legacy - I build, grow, and serve. Investing my efforts in actions that resonate beyond the present, creating lasting, positive impact.

Lord, please give me the strength to do these things, and the faith to trust that you will fulfill your word and bless me, the works of my hands, and my house mightily.

Holy Spirit I surrender to You, please lead me, amen."

By transforming the WayMaker code into a proclamation, and then building upon it as a foundation for my own life goals, this practice has created a living document, a hypothesis and theory in the form of a working draft from which I evaluate my actions, fortify myself for the day ahead, and seek to further align myself with that which I desire to be.

APPLICATION CHECK

As you reflect on the WayMaker Code and its tenets, consider how they manifest in your daily life. This Application Check aims to transition from intellectual understanding to practical application, ensuring that the Code's principles are not just ideas but are lived and experienced.

1. Reflect on a recent instance where you lived by the WayMaker Code. What was the outcome, and what did you learn about yourself?

2. Identify one tenet of the WayMaker Code that resonates with you the least. What is one specific habit or behavior you can adopt to embody this tenet more fully?

3. Look back over the past month. What evidence—actions, decisions, or changes—demonstrates that you are truly internalizing the WayMaker Code?

CHAPTER 4:

DAILY RITUAL - THE OPENING STATEMENT

It is my opinion that the most impactful examples are provided by those who are actually executing the behavior in question. Instead of exploring each element of the WayMaker Code or Proclamation theoretically, we will explore each element through the lens of my daily meditation ritual, why I find value in it on a personal level, and how you can create value that aligns with your personal ideals in a manner that supports you.

To start, I have a very intentional section that opens prior to directly stating the modified tenants of the WayMaker Proclamation. Let us explore its elements, and the reason I have selected them to this point. The first element is:

"Lord, I lay down the troubles and burdens of my heart, the fears, and insecurities, so that you may remove them by your own hand and instruct my actions. Please forgive me for where I have sinned and help me to grow stronger and healthier so that I may better serve You, purify me, so that I may walk with You and receive your Spirit, please pour out Your favor and Your Holy Spirit on my house and me."

This passage signifies humility and relinquished control for that which is outside of my ability to directly influence. Furthermore, it allows me to provide myself the grace in the highly iterative and cyclical growth trajectory that I believe we as humans experience.

The word "sin" means to miss the "mark" or target, and as I ask for forgiveness, I ask for it from that which I believe has called me to lead a maximized life as well as myself. The acceptance of my fallibility, followed by the grounding of self in growth, health, and manifestation of favor help to focus my mind to acknowledge and learn from my failings and then immediately press into correcting my trajectory for the day in alignment with my long-term goals.

> *"Please help me to think, deeply, intuitively, and well, please grant me wisdom and insight far beyond my mortal form. Please grant me the courage to change what is in my control, the serenity to accept that which is not, and the wisdom to discern between the two. Please enable further levels of freedom, empowerment, influence, purpose, and peace."*

There is that which we know that which we know we do not know, and that which we do not know that we do not know it. Given this I find it helpful to remind myself to think deeply and with great intention, pursuing wisdom. Then I incorporate an ancient serenity prayer that I find beautiful, and directly tie it to my insatiable desire for freedom born from responsibility and capability.

> *"Please teach me how to give of myself open and freely, and how to receive in kind. Please safeguard my family, myself, and my mind."*

I think that a significant amount of skill is involved in both offering and accepting generosity. Reminding myself to cultivate these skills daily is crucial to the way I aspire to lead my life. The statement on safeguarding my family, self, and mind help me to remember that though there is much beauty in this world, I must be on guard, as there are threats, and we must remain vigilant.

> *"I commit myself to You Lord, and I commit my works to You Lord so that all that I do may honor You. Given this, I proclaim the following as truth so that Your will may be done, and that I may honor You:"*

I believe that there is a higher power as well as a near unattainable ideal form of self. This statement anchors me in the recognition of this truth and inspires me to actively pursue an honorable life.

Once you have defined your ideals, I highly recommend that you write an intentional opening statement that helps to ground and align you to the proclamation that follows. If you are at a loss on where to begin such a statement, I would propose that something as simple as the following will provide a sufficient starting point. From there you will have the ability to build and refine your statement over time as you walk through it day by day.

A STARTING PLACE FOR YOUR DAILY MEDITATION RITUAL

"I will cultivate the courage to change what is in my control, the serenity to accept that which is not, and the wisdom to discern between the two. Now I proclaim the following over my life:"

CHAPTER 5:

LIVE INTENTIONALLY

> *"I Live Intentionally - I choose to be present in each moment. I align my actions with my deepest values, consistently striving for personal excellence and meaningful impact."*

The first tenet of the WayMaker Proclamation, presented here in italics, is a guiding principle for me. Included with it, in the standard font, you will find the adaptations I have made for my daily ritual. Note that I carry this format throughout the remaining chapters.

I think that without intentional thought and action, it is foolish to expect things to magically fall into place. To practice this, I state that I am making the choice to both be present in each moment, and purposeful in that which I do.

> *"I hold on to the outcome loosely but hold to the path fervently."*

Knowledge comes in layers. At the basic level, there is awareness of something. Beyond that lies a competent understanding. The deepest layer is experiential knowledge—profound, thorough, and impactful. The wisdom of holding the outcome lightly and the path tightly was learned through this deepest form of knowledge. It has been one of the most significant revelations of my life. It taught me to distinguish between what I can influence and what I can only react to. Embracing this insight has brought me a greater sense of peace, even while navigating through times of intense chaos and adversity.

> *"I rejoice in doing what others refuse to do, so that I may do that which others are incapable of doing. And as I stand in the gap, I call others forward and equip them to do the same."*

I do not just do the things others refuse to do; I choose to rejoice in doing them. Why? So that I can build within myself the capability to equip others to do the same.

This powerfully reminds me that I am intentionally, and freely choosing to live my life in the way that I am as well as why I am doing it. Which is especially helpful given that I am often conducting this meditation prior to 4:00 AM in the morning, when sleepiness and fatigue are at their greatest.

CHAPTER 6:

CULTIVATE CURIOSITY

> *"I Cultivate Curiosity - I seek the thrill of the unknown with eager questions and an open mind."*

Due to the intentional manner in which I engineered my opening statement, I did not assess a need to modify this tenant. Curiosity is the powerful catalyst that helps to inspire a continuous growth posture to the world.

I see learning as the thrill, curiosity as the fuel, and questions as the vehicle to explore and learn, thus opening my mind to greater understanding and that which I have yet to discover. I deeply love the playful impactfulness that this tenant evokes and seek to see the world as if through the eyes of a child.

This has greatly improved the quality of my life as I firmly think that the day that we stop learning, is the day that we begin to die.

Additionally, I maintain that all things of value can endure scrutiny. Valuable entities will prove their worth, becoming more esteemed as they are questioned. Conversely, falsehoods will unravel under examination, revealing any supposed value as illusory. While discovering these truths may be distressing, I embrace the authenticity and reconstruct my understanding and life around it rather than clinging to comforting deceptions. Put more lightheartedly, no 'sacred cow' exists, meaning no idea or belief should be exempt from critical evaluation.

A few examples that illustrate the value of this tenant in my life are:

1. Challenging and freeing myself from "sunk cost fallacies". I have left companies that I have worked with after challenging a "sacred cow", or idea held beyond reproach, to only find that it was untrue and that no one was willing to rectify it.

2. The resilience to stumble, rise, and persistently experiment has significantly expanded my knowledge across various fields, including Artificial Intelligence. It is tempting to abandon endeavors like AI after initial disappointing outcomes. However, I find it far more fulfilling to sustain my curiosity and diligently investigate the potential benefits before hastily dismissing them as valueless.

3. Build it as you go: Experimentation, pursuing the question "how might I unleash human potential?" and wondering how I can build strong community around the WayMaker Philosophy has led to the creation of the WayMaker Community. This community is a social experiment-style hypothesis that, in its first year, has evolved substantially because of the curiosity-inspired questions mentioned above.

CHAPTER 7:

PURSUE WISDOM

> *"**I Pursue Wisdom** - I nurture a growth mindset, relentlessly seeking knowledge and insight, and learning from both success and failure."*

Upon initial observation, this principle might seem repetitive. However, it embodies subtle yet significant differences from previous principles, which serve to sharpen the impact of this declaration.

Wisdom is more than knowledge, especially when you are willing to learn from both your successes and your failures. Here is a fun example - is a tomato a vegetable or a fruit? Hopefully you know that a tomato is a fruit, if not then surprise! However, wisdom takes it further, as wisdom would be to understand that despite a tomato being a fruit, you should not put it in a fruit salad.

Though this example is intentionally simplistic, it effectively illustrates the larger idea. A profound distinction exists between Wisdom, akin to art, and Knowledge, akin to science. In the pursuit of wisdom, we derive lessons from both triumphs and setbacks, integrating hands-on experience with scholarly understanding. We grasp not only the rigid rules but also the fundamental reasons behind them, acknowledging the many nuances of reality, beyond mere black and white. This nuanced comprehension enhances our ability to navigate life's complexities.

CHAPTER 8:

UPHOLD TRUTH

"I Uphold Truth - I speak the truth with deliberate intentionality, so that each word precisely relays the meaning and value that I intend for it to relay, and so my yes means yes and my no means no. Furthermore, I prioritize forthrightness, openly admitting my mistakes, and fostering integrity in every action and interaction."

What is truth? Defining it is challenging, but it seems to me that actively seeking wisdom and fostering curiosity are reliable methods for navigating the world. This approach allows for a continuous exploration and understanding of the ever-evolving nature of truth. As a strong advocate of the scientific method, I believe in rigorously testing ideas, upholding those that withstand scrutiny, and abandoning those that falter. Simultaneously, I strive to keep an open mind and avoid clinging to any ideas that resist critical examination, a principle we explored in chapter 6.

I emphasize this because unchallenged beliefs or perceived 'truths' can lead to disastrous outcomes. I am committed to speaking the truth as I perceive it, to the fullest extent of my abilities. I aim to express only what strengthens me, even if it is uncomfortable. I diligently strive to comprehend what I advocate for, especially in avoiding the easy way out during high-stakes or contentious situations.

When I discover a belief that I have held is incorrect, I change my position. This is necessary, no matter how foundational the belief, how difficult the change, or how much of a personal crisis it may create. I consider it a fundamental duty to continually test our convictions and to champion them only as long as they remain true.

I THINK, I FEEL, AND I BELIEVE

Exploring the subtle differences between the phrases 'I think,' 'I feel,' and 'I believe' is crucial in any discourse on truth. While each expression may represent an aspect of truth, they also have the potential to mislead us unintentionally, as they each stem from fundamentally different origins.

Some examples:

1. **I Feel:** I can feel like someone attempted to hurt me on purpose, and perhaps they did. But I will not know until I ask and verify their intent. If they did have malicious intent, then my feelings were accurate. However, if they did not, then my feelings lied to me. Given this I look to emotion as a neutral teacher, extending its hand in invitation to seek understanding into why I am interpreting the scenario at hand in the manner that I am.

2. **I Think:** Especially when discussing contrasting ideas in the realm of business, I think that stating your opinion as a manner of intentional thought is far more effective than stating that you feel a certain way about a decision that needs to be made. We will not explore this concept exhaustively, however, a great way to bridge the gap when thought and emotion are at odds is to state each precisely.

3. **I Believe:** Belief represents a unique, highly specific decision that ought to be made with great intention. Faith is to believe in that which cannot yet be seen or proven. Many wars have been fought over clashing beliefs born of uncompromising faith. Yet I also think belief holds value when handled carefully.

4. We cannot definitively prove whether God or other higher powers exist. I have explored extensively, trying to validate or disprove such existence. After years of seeking evidence, I remain unsatisfied - unable to conclusively prove or disprove a higher power. However, intuition suggests there is more beyond mortal comprehension. Given this, I believe something greater exists which I cannot yet fully explain or quantify. I choose to believe while acknowledging this belief remains grounded in faith rather than facts. It is subject to ongoing scrutiny as I continue seeking truth.

5. I am uninterested in persuading others as this represents my personal conviction after wrestling to align evidence, logic, and experience in my specific life. We each must thoughtfully shape our own ideological positions on such matters. But regardless of specific beliefs, we should hold them loosely as we uphold truth as a lifelong, evolving pursuit of understanding.

6. **Methods of Governing a Nation – A Discernment Exercise:** Applying the principles of 'I think,' 'I believe,' and 'I feel,' let us explore a real-world example of these concepts in action: the governance of nations. This final example contrasts the ideologies of Democracy and Communism. Both are imperfect, yet the last 150 years have starkly differentiated their outcomes. Democracy, with all its flaws, has generally fostered individual sovereignty, wealth, and resilience. In contrast, Communism has directly led to the deaths of tens of millions and widespread suffering. The overwhelming evidence indicates that democracy facilitates prosperity and freedom, while communism has repeatedly resulted in oppression and devastation. Despite any theoretical merits communism may claim, its real-world applications have proven catastrophically inferior. The prospect of future communist experiments offers little appeal given the grave historical consequences. Additionally, I think that our strength and prosperity are intrinsically linked to individual liberty. I firmly believe that as humans, we thrive when navigating life's complexities, conflicts, and pains from a stance of personal responsibility and freedom, rather than relinquishing these duties to an authoritative regime.

I hope that these examples help to illustrate the distinction between statements such as "I think", "I feel", and "I believe". Furthermore, given the complexity, lack of certifiable proof, and many shades of grey that encompass making any form of a decision, I hope that I have thoroughly illustrated the great intention that is beneficial to deploy in our thought and speech as we navigate this life.

It is due to this, that I intentionally choose to speak the truth, to the best of my ability, while holding loosely to that which I believe. I make it a point to admit when I am wrong, especially after gaining better information. I strive for clarity in my communication, ensuring that 'yes' and 'no' are unequivocal. Throughout life's journey, I aim to constantly refine my understanding of truth and let go of falsehoods.

> *"I remember that what I do speaks so loudly that no one can hear what I say..."*

This addition is critical because action always speaks louder than words. Yes, there are times were choosing to speak is an intentional act, and within the act of speaking you display your character. But reflecting on the thread of thought, speech, and action being the ingredients that make up an individual, what we do often is the most powerful example of who we are.

An example of this can be pulled from reflecting on my own behavior, and how my children have responded. For years I spoke about discipline, creating value, and treating others well. Yet, in the little time that I was home, they saw me drink more than anything else.

So, what did they do? They would pretend to drink to connect with me.

Now, and for the past few years, I have drunk little, am home far more, and choose to spend my time writing, podcasting, reading, building, and investing in those around me. So how do my children play now?

They pretend to podcast, to write books, to be businessmen.

Yes, my rhetoric has improved, but nowhere near as dramatically as the overwhelming preponderance of my actions. Additionally, now that my actions align with my words, that which I say carries far more authority as my children are more receptive to listening. What a powerful barometer. If you are curious as to the quality of your character, watch how those closest to you portray you, and if you have children, watch them play.

> *"And what I do in private, is written on my soul. Given this I pause and weigh my actions so that my decisions make me stronger."*

This final element is my daily reminder to strengthen my integrity. As I believe that our private actions are what strengthen or weaken our character and self-perception.

How do we use this to our advantage?

With patience and long suffering, we change the manner in which we behave in private so that it aligns with our ideals, until our actions in front of others speak so loudly, they begin to hear what we say.

APPLICATION CHECK

Truth is a cornerstone of character and integrity. This Application Check invites you to explore your personal relationship with truth, examining how it aligns with your actions and how it shapes your understanding of yourself and the world around you.

1. Think of a recent situation where your commitment to truth was challenged. How did you respond, and what did it reveal about your character?

2. Identify a personal "truth" or belief that may need re-examination. What steps can you take to challenge and refine this belief?

3. Consider the environments you frequent (work, family, community). How can you foster spaces that uphold truth and reject deceit or dishonesty?

CHAPTER 9:

BE RELENTLESS

> *"**I Am Relentless** - I exercise extraordinary violence of action, consistently chasing my goals, I overcome obstacles with unwavering tenacity, and enduring resolve."*

I went into great depth concerning the power of relentless action, consistency and Sisu as catalysts for progress in my first book "Be Relentless: If the obstacle is the way, then we must be WayMakers". I firmly believe that it is relentless, decisive action applied over a long-time horizon that creates influential leaders, community builders, and world shapers; people I call WayMakers.

Proclaiming this daily reminds me where I have come from, and what it costs to continue to evolve as I forge forward.

Let us continue to cultivate such disciplined drive and be among the select few who choose to live life with eyes wide open, stepping out of the spectators' seats and into the proverbial arena.

"It is not the critic who counts, not the man who points out how the strong man stumbles or where the doer of deeds could have done better. The credit belongs to the man who is actually in the arena, whose face is marred by dust and sweat and blood, who strives valiantly, who errs and comes up short again and again, because there is no effort without error or shortcoming, but who knows the great enthusiasms, the great devotions, who spends himself in a worthy cause; who, at the best, knows, in the end, the triumph of high achievement, and who, at the worst, if he fails, at least he fails while daring greatly, so that his place shall never be with those cold and timid souls who knew neither victory nor defeat."

- THEODORE ROOSEVELT

To stay the course, despite the overabundance of critics and adversity, and despite the oftentimes absent fruits of our labor, you do not need to endure alone. It is true that no one is coming to save you, but it is equally true that we are stronger when we work, fight, live, and love in a tightly interconnected community.

CHAPTER 10:

FORGE COURAGE

"I Forge Courage - *Knowing that bravery is a choice, I choose to take decisive action in the face of adversity. I embrace discomfort and push beyond my current limits to grow stronger. I choose to lead well."*

Courage is not the absence of fear, but action despite it. In the same way, leadership, whether it is leading oneself, family, community, or further, is about choosing to take deliberate actions that reflect the responsibility of making a difference, in line with one's goals. A beautiful, eloquent, and timeless expression of this is Rudyard Kipling's poem "If".

> If you can keep your head when all about you
> Are losing theirs and blaming it on you,
> If you can trust yourself when all men doubt you,
> But make allowance for their doubting too;
> If you can wait and not be tired by waiting,
> Or being lied about, don't deal in lies,
> Or being hated, don't give way to hating,
> And yet don't look too good, nor talk too wise:
>
> If you can dream—and not make dreams your master;
> If you can think—and not make thoughts your aim;
> If you can meet with Triumph and Disaster
> And treat those two impostors just the same;
> If you can bear to hear the truth you've spoken
> Twisted by knaves to make a trap for fools,
> Or watch the things you gave your life to, broken,
> And stoop and build 'em up with worn-out tools:
>
> If you can make one heap of all your winnings
> And risk it on one turn of pitch-and-toss,
> And lose, and start again at your beginnings
> And never breathe a word about your loss;
> If you can force your heart and nerve and sinew
> To serve your turn long after they are gone,
> And so hold on when there is nothing in you
> Except the Will which says to them: 'Hold on!'
>
> If you can talk with crowds and keep your virtue,
> Or walk with Kings—nor lose the common touch,
> If neither foes nor loving friends can hurt you,
> If all men count with you, but none too much;
> If you can fill the unforgiving minute
> With sixty seconds' worth of distance run,
> Yours is the Earth and everything that's in it,
> And—which is more—you'll be a Man, my son!

APPLICATION CHECK

Courage is not the absence of fear but the victory over it. This Application Check is an opportunity to confront your fears, big or small, and to recognize and celebrate the courage within yourself and in others.

1. Identify something you have been avoiding due to fear. What is one small step you can take towards it? What barriers do you need to overcome to make this step?

2. Reflect on a recent act of courage, either by you or someone else. How did it impact you or others? How can you acknowledge and celebrate such acts more regularly?

3. Consider an area of your life (work, family, hobbies) where you have been playing it safe. How can you bring more courage into this area?

CHAPTER 11:

EMBODY SISU

"I Embody Sisu - I foster resilience in the face of adversity. I lead by example and transform challenges into opportunities for growth."

There is good in everything if only we have the courage to find it, the strength to utilize it, and the resilience to sustain ourselves on it. Life is often challenging and rarely pleasurable. When we are happy, acquiring what we desire, and the days are sweet we ought to cherish it.

The rest of the time I cultivate and rely on Sisu. Sisu to me embodies the American spirit, the idea of fighting for freedom, of winning despite being the underdog, and ultimately being indomitable.

This Finnish concept is a universal capacity that we all share, and one that so powerfully captures much of what I work to embody that it is a consistent thread throughout my work, businesses, and life. It also is an invitation.

"Sisu begins where grit ends. Sisu represents dauntless determination, courage, and grit in the face of extreme adversity. It is an action based personal ownership mindset which enables individuals to reach beyond their present limitations, take action against all odds, and transform barriers into frontiers of opportunity."

I understand that this idea can come across as nice on paper, but how does it perform when applied?

The concept of Sisu originated in Finland, where the harsh climate and war-ridden history forced stoic determination. Sisu empowered ordinary citizens to endure immense suffering while safeguarding national identity.

In my own life, I cultivate Sisu by waking up early (typically before 4:00 am), taking occasional ice baths, and conducting physical training daily.

These core routines condition mental resilience to find opportunity when situations appear bleakest.

Examples include:

1. When injuries threatened athletic goals, I persevered through pain to strengthen supportive muscle groups and adjust technique rather than accept defeat.

2. When a project fails despite fervent efforts, I force myself to identify lessons that enhance future success instead of wallowing in disappointment.

3. When cancelled plans free up an evening, I pour that time into nurturing my marriage despite desiring leisure with other friends.

In these ways, Sisu encourages us to change our perspective from noticing what is missing to recognizing the opportunities that lie before us for progress.

CHAPTER 12:

FOSTER UNITY

> *"**I Foster Unity** - I cultivate compassion and seek understanding. I respond with intention. I believe that together, we are stronger, and our progress is amplified when we work together."*

We have already delved deeply into two of the concepts presented at the start of this tenet. Yet, their true importance emerges when we approach them with the aim of fostering compassion and understanding, rather than hardening ourselves and erecting barriers.

Our world is filled with an unending list of reasons to close ourselves off, erect barriers, and sow dissention. But it does not have to be this way.

Instead of focusing on what divides us, if we invest our efforts in what unifies us then we position ourselves to receive a multitude of benefits.

> *"I choose LOVE and I breathe in gratitude."*

Love and gratitude are manifested through intentional thought, word, and action. You do not believe me? For the next month, write down 15 things that you are grateful for (i.e. Things you would miss or be sad if they disappeared). Then tell me what has changed concerning how you think and feel after that month.

I state this daily so that I never forget it, and as I read "breathe in gratitude" I take a literal deep breath and focus on the sensation. To be alive is a gift!

> *"I seek to cultivate a vibrant life of love with Lindsey, my bride, and pursue her with fresh eyes, elation, and wonder. I cherish her and choose to love her more deeply, today, and I discipline my mind and body such that she is my only source of satisfaction, otherwise I maintain my strength."*

They say that the grass is always greener on the other side, and perhaps this is because we cannot see the flaws from where we sit when we gaze enviously at what is outside of our reach. I propose that the grass is greenest where we water, weed and tend to it. Given this belief, I work diligently to pursue the heart of my bride, build hedges of protection around our marriage, and ground myself in this choice daily. At the time of writing this, we have been blessed with over a decade's worth of marriage, and through this practice I strive to safeguard many more, brighter decades ahead.

> *"I cultivate control over the expression of my emotions, thoughts, and my voice as I instruct my sons, through my example and my word. I choose to cherish my time with them and remember that each moment is a gift."*

There is an adage that the cobbler's children often go without shoes. The above addition to my daily meditative ritual helps to ground me in working from the self-outward, as opposed to the world inward.

This is critical. It is far too often that we hear of successful businessmen whose homes are in shambles.

What do I have to gain if I am so mission focused that I forget to properly tend to those who rely on me most?

Let it never be. The work outside of my home must never be allowed overshadow my responsibility within it.

Furthermore, temperance, self-restraint, and mastery of self have never proven more necessary than in molding my children into young men. If I yell, they yell. If I speak softly, they speak softly. It is my responsibility to master my emotions and to teach them how to love, show restraint, compassion, and good judgement. It is their reflection of me that demonstrates my imperfections and strengths, that helps to strengthen me as I continue to pursue a better version of self for their benefit.

Reminding oneself of such responsibilities is critical to not allow them to fade outside of the forefront of our mind. That which we do not cultivate, does not grow, or worse, grows in far worse ways then we ever intended.

HOW CAN YOU CREATE A MORE POSITIVE INFLUENCE IN YOURSELF AS YOU WORK TO FOSTER UNITY?

WHO IS WATCHING YOU?

CHAPTER 13:

CHAMPION FREEDOM

> *"I Champion Freedom - Freedom comes at a price. Therefore, I take responsibility for safeguarding it and dedicate efforts to cultivate a world where liberty flourishes."*

Unless you have experienced or witnessed oppression it is hard to fully grasp the joy and gift that freedom is. When I commissioned as an officer in the Army, I took an oath to safeguard freedom and uphold the constitution. An oath that I am bound to today, despite no longer being a soldier. It is one of two oaths I have taken throughout my life, the other occurred when I married my bride.

The oath that I swore when entering service was to uphold the constitution, not a president or a political affiliation. It is the constitution that does a beautiful job to help safeguard individual liberty above all else, which is no simple task and will always require many to stand in the gap and protect it so that others may benefit from the opportunity it provides.

I continue to remind myself of my duty to my fellow man. I reflect on those I love who lost their lives as they fought to safeguard our freedom. I think of those who continue to serve and fight today for the same. I think of those who advocate the progression of freedom in their home with their children, in their community with their peers, and globally, as we work to extend the opportunity for others to live in the freedom born prosperity that sweetens our lives.

Furthermore, it is my belief that each of us is responsible for safeguarding and cultivating a world where liberty flourishes. This responsibility spans both military and civic sectors, for freedom lives where people understand the prosperity that it creates. Every citizen fortunate enough to have won the birth lottery and live in a free country can work to safeguard and progress liberty through thought, speech, and action.

We must not waste this opportunity.

We must not allow those who have died in our place to die in vain.

We degrade liberty absent individual courage yet only retain it through common effort.

I will do my part, proclaim such daily, and align my actions accordingly.

WILL YOU?

DEFINING FREEDOM

Freedom begins where compliance ends. Freedom represents the courage to think and act independently, to cultivate personal growth unhindered by external control. It is a mindset of self-ownership that rejects barriers and limitations, instead exercising one's faculties to take purposeful action.

True freedom acknowledges the liberty of others. It persists through struggle and transcends circumstances through indomitable determination. Freedom depends on the individual strength to accept consequences and responsibility for one's choices and is predicated upon the individual's decision to bear up under the weight of their discipline-born responsibilities.

Freedom grants individuals' sovereignty over their lives. It unleashes personal potential and guards the human spirit against restraint. Freedom catalyzes creativity, issue resolution, and the autonomous capacity to define one's own purpose. It echoes the irrepressible life force that strives forward under adversity and expands in proportion to resistance.

WE ARE ONLY AS STRONG, AS WE ARE INDIVIDUALLY FREE.

APPLICATION CHECK

Freedom and liberty are foundational yet require constant vigilance and commitment. This Application Check encourages you to consider your role in nurturing and protecting these values, both in your personal life and in the broader community.

1. Reflect on a recent news event or policy change related to the infringement of individual freedom. What are its implications, and how does it resonate with your values?

2. What actions can you take to safeguard freedom and individual liberty? Where might you be complacent about infringements on core freedoms?

3. Identify one action you can take this month to promote and protect freedoms in your community or sphere of influence.

CHAPTER 14:

BUILD LEGACY

*"**I Build Legacy** - I build, grow, and serve. Investing my efforts in actions that resonate beyond the present, creating lasting, positive impact."*

What do the following have in common?

David Brookes concept of "Second Mountain Pursuits".

Simon Sinek's concept of the "Infinite Game".

The concept, popular in the veteran community of ones "Second Mission".

The ancient desire for honor and glory.

The modern desire for respect and love.

These concepts all share a central theme, that those who are working toward and achieving these ideas are creating impact that extends far beyond themselves.

"A society grows great when old men plant trees in whose shade they know they shall never sit."

- GREEK PARABLE

By taking daily action that embodies our discussion thus far, we further refine our intentions. This prepares a world where not just our children, but their children too, will thrive.

This is why I think that every action that I take, now, matters. It is why I write and podcast, this is why I work to create value, build strong community, and steward successful businesses.

Think beyond this moment.

WHAT CAN YOU CONTRIBUTE TO THE WORLD THAT WILL LEAVE IT BETTER THAN WHEN YOU WERE BORN INTO IT?

HOW DO YOU PUT THIS INTO ACTION NOW?

CHAPTER 15:

COMPLETING THE DAILY RITUAL

"Lord, please give me the strength to do these things, and the faith to trust that you will fulfill your word and bless me, the works of my hands, and my house mightily.

Holy Spirit I surrender to You, please lead me, amen."

Similar to the serenity prayer and the beginning of my daily ritual, these final words reinforce my determination to bring my declarations to life today. They enable me to concentrate on what I can control, respond intentionally to what I cannot, and move forward with peace.

This ritual, rooted in humility, protected by freedom, and driven by a creative desire, strengthens my journey to improve as a WayMaker and grow into a better man.

A great suggestion to close your daily ritual is:

"And now I rise and will put these things into action."

THEN GO FORTH AND DO IT.

CHAPTER 16:

YOUR LIFE LIVED FOR MORE THAN SELF

Our freedom has been secured by the sacrifices of great individuals, who have given us the power to forge a transformative future. Our current freedom and prosperity were born from the unwavering bravery of those who stood against tyranny. They toiled, envisioning a world without the chains of the impossible.

To be indifferent or to chase only selfish ends is to dishonor this heritage. The freedom, bought at such a high price, requires our diligent care, lest it fades away. The cost of maintaining liberty is far less than the cost of enduring subjugation. Yet, we too often take for granted this dearly won treasure.

The WayMaker Code calls us to a higher purpose, beyond hollow successes measured in vanity. We forge forward so that those who come after us will continue to inherit the same freedom born opportunity that we have so greatly benefited from, even as we choose to work to progress it.

The start of the journey, its continuation and its end, all stem from care for those whom we love in juxtaposition and mutual support to our relationship with self.

Connection, love, gratitude, and the resolve to live for those we love define our unique and powerful nature as a species. By fostering inner peace and demonstrating unwavering strength, we enhance our collective well-being.

The true measure of a life is the echo left in its wake—whether we cravenly consume comforts and squander our time, or become the WayMakers who build a brighter tomorrow, today. The choice remains ours, for beyond the self lies the infinite game: our legacy, crafted through service now so that generations may flourish because we did not falter.

This is not a short game.

The Path of the WayMaker is a lifelong journey—one of sacrifice, self-cultivation, and an unrelenting resolve to be a part of the solution our world so desperately needs.

They say freedom can be lost within one generation. This is true.

BUT AS LONG AS THERE ARE WAYMAKERS, THIS FATE WILL NEVER COME TO PASS.

APPLICATION CHECK

As we part ways for now, it is time to consider the legacy you will leave behind. This Application Check aims to equip you towards intentional living, focusing on the relationships and contributions that truly matter.

1. Reflect on the feedback you have received from friends and family. Identify one area for improvement in how you receive and act on this feedback.

2. Think about the legacy you want to leave in one aspect of your life (personal, professional, community). What are the first three steps you can take towards this legacy?

3. What is one "legacy experiment" (something you can create or initiate) that you can start now? How does it reflect your values and aspirations, and what commitment will it require from you?

PUTTING IT INTO ACTION

We have now thoroughly examined the WayMaker Code, transformed it into a Proclamation, and thoroughly explored my personal daily meditative ritual as well as the why behind each element of it. Now it is time for you to do the same for yourself. Here is a baseline template that draws on everything we have discussed to this point:

"I will cultivate the courage to change that which is in my control, the serenity to accept that which is not, and the wisdom to discern between the two. Now I proclaim the following over my life:

I Live Intentionally - I align my actions with my deepest values, consistently striving for personal excellence and meaningful impact.

I Cultivate Curiosity - I seek the thrill of the unknown with eager questions and an open mind.

I Pursue Wisdom - I nurture a growth mindset, relentlessly seeking knowledge and insight, and learning from both success and failure.

I Uphold Truth - I prioritize forthrightness, openly admit my mistakes, and foster integrity in every action and interaction.

I Am Relentless - I consistently chase my goals, overcoming obstacles with unwavering tenacity, and enduring resolve.

I Forge Courage - Knowing that bravery is a choice, I choose to take decisive action in the face of adversity. I embrace discomfort and push beyond my current limits to grow stronger.

I Embody Sisu - I foster resilience in the face of adversity. I lead by example and transform challenges into opportunities for growth.

I Foster Unity - I cultivate compassion and seek understanding. Together, we are stronger, and our progress is amplified when we work together.

I Champion Freedom - Freedom comes at a price. Therefore, I take responsibility for safeguarding it and dedicate efforts to cultivate a world where liberty flourishes.

I Build Legacy - I invest my efforts in actions that resonate beyond the present, creating lasting, positive impact.

Now, as I rise, I will put these truths into relentless action as I Forge Forward."

AFTERWORD

"Be Relentless: If the obstacle is the way, then we must be WayMakers" embodies an invitation to lead a maximized life and become a WayMaker.

This book, "Forge Forward: Your Freedom is Hard Earned" explores what occurs once you become a WayMaker, and how to fortify yourself as you continue to grow through the infinite yet fleeting flash that is life. My hope is that it inspires thought and offers tangible, thought-provoking insights to help you stay on the path as we all travel together.

I envision the continuation of this work focusing on the concept of a "Fellowship of Freemen". In which the culmination of the ideas discussed thus far, applied in intentional forms of community, help to foster growth, value creation, and strong communities across our country and perhaps even the world. These ideas and this work are being tested within the WayMaker Community. But for now, as you continue to stay the course as a WayMaker, dare to build something so powerful, that when you reflect upon the work of your hands you will realize that it built you.

COURAGE

BY JONATHAN MAYO

The one who dreams yet will not sleep,
Faces pain with courage deep,
Words aligned in truth's bright rays,
Marching forth through trial's haze.

With discipline, their path is drawn,
Toward a purpose that shines with dawn,
Each day in body and mind they train,
Leaving past comforts, embracing gain.

In community, their bonds grow strong,
Together standing where they belong,
They lift their light for all to see,
Ensuring freedom's flame burns free.

Living intentional, relentless, unbound,
They free potential where it is found,
Conquering obstacles, they transform the night,
WayMakers in the storm, becoming the light.

Though we rage against the fading day,
Their resolve shines in the fray,
Weaving a legacy, strong and spread,
Honoring the path where their courage led.

www.ingramcontent.com/pod-product-compliance
Lightning Source LLC
Chambersburg PA
CBHW062120080426
42734CB00012B/2932